MATH
TO KNOW
Parent Guide

EDUCATION GROUP
A Houghton Mifflin Company

Acknowledgments

We gratefully acknowledge the following parents who helped make *Math to Know* a reality.

Marianne Knowles
Andover, MA

Sandra Laquidara
Andover, MA

Julie Mendonca
Lowell, MA.

Writing: Justine Dunn
Editorial: Carol DeBold, Justine Dunn, Susan Rogalski
Design Management: Richard Spencer
Production Management: Evelyn Curley
Design and Production: Bill SMITH STUDIO
Marketing: Lisa Bingen
Illustration: Scott Ritchie
Part Opener Illustrations: Joe Spooner

Printed in the United States of America

International Standard Book Number: 0-669-50042-9

1 2 3 4 5 6 7 8 9 10 RRD 07 06 05 04 03

Visit our website: www.greatsource.com

CONTENTS

INTRODUCTION

As a parent, you want to do what is best for your child. Sometimes when it comes to helping your child with math, you may not be sure what "best" is. *How much help should I give? What if I don't remember (or recognize) some of the math I learned in school? How can I help my child with tests? How can I make sure that math is interesting and fun rather than frightening to my child? How do I communicate with the teacher?* This booklet will answer these and many more questions you may have as it helps you use *Math to Know* with your child.

A successful parent often plays many roles in the process of parenting. Let's look at some of the roles you will need to play in order to best help your child learn mathematics.

Tutor

As a tutor, you can help with the practice and memorization that are part of getting a firm grasp on many math topics. You can also help your child learn about math topics he or she may have had trouble understanding at school. *Math to Know* is a handbook which covers all of the topics taught in grades three and four and reviews topics from previous grades. For most types of math problems, you will find several different ways to find the answer. You should probably start with the way your child was taught at school, but you might find one of the other ways works better.

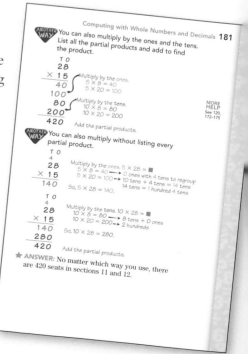

Role Model

Make your child aware of how often you use math in everyday life, whether it is comparing prices in a grocery store, balancing your checkbook, setting up a newly-purchased toy, or figuring out game scores. When you need to stop and think about a problem before solving it, share your thinking. Let your child know that some problems are harder than others and that means spending a little time on them and double-checking your work. Even if you did not like or succeed in math when you were in school, try to keep your attitude positive. You don't want to accidentally give the impression that it's OK for your child to do poorly in math.

Resource

Some children may be very independent. That is a good thing, though you may want to check your child's work just to be sure he or she really does not need help. Give your child the handbook, *Math to Know,* and be sure he or she knows you are ready to help.

Partner to the teacher

Your child's teacher spends about six hours a day, five days a week with your child. He or she probably knows your child quite well. But, remember, you've been with your child a lot longer and have had many more chances to work one-on-one. There may be things the teacher doesn't know about your child. Maybe your child learns better by doing an activity than by reading about it in a book, or perhaps your child learns best by listening.

It is important to provide the teacher with as much information about your child as you can. It is also important for you to know what is being taught, so that you can reinforce the curriculum at home. Remember, you and the teacher have the same goal: to help your child learn. Your role as partner to the teacher may be as important as your role as advocate for your child.

This booklet will provide you with answers to many of your questions about helping your child with math. The handbook, *Math to Know,* will supply you with everything you need to know about the mathematics taught in grades three and four. This booklet and the handbook together will give you all the tools you need to successfully play the roles of tutor, role model, resource, and partner to the teacher.

Creating a Good Learning
ENVIRONMENT

When it comes to homework, many children need a little encouragement from their parents. Make homework part of your children's regular routine. Help them find the best location in your home for doing their homework and be sure they have all the tools they need.

Creating a Good Learning
ENVIRONMENT

Q: *When my children come home from school, they need a break. Then after a break, they don't have what it takes to get started again. They often end up doing their homework late at night or not at all. What would you suggest?*

A: When children come home from school, they do need a break. Set a specified time for the break—30 minutes should be long enough. Use a timer if you like. Then help your child get started. Allow short breaks during homework time. A five-minute break every 20 minutes works well.

Homework needs to be part of a routine. It isn't always possible to have exactly the same schedule, because of outside activities, but let your children know that homework time starts, say, 30 minutes after getting home or 10 minutes after dinner. If children wait until late at night to do homework, they usually don't have the level of concentration that they need. Also, since it isn't always easy to predict how long an assignment may take, they may not finish before bedtime. If homework seems to be taking too much time, check with your children's teachers about how long it <u>should</u> be taking.

A: Be sure she has a place that is well lit with lots of room for her to spread out. It's probably best for her to sit at a desk or table, but we've heard of students who feel more comfortable at the kitchen counter or on the floor. If possible, she should not be too far away from you, so that you can answer her questions, help her stay focused, and provide help if she needs it. The homework place should be as free from distractions as possible. Your daughter shouldn't be disturbed by the television or other members of the household. Sometimes, you can accomplish this with a soothing music CD and earphones.

Q: *What kinds of supplies should my son have at hand?*

A: Always have a good supply of paper (including graph paper), pencils, a good pencil sharpener, and erasers close at hand. Some assignments may require rulers, so have an inch ruler and a centimeter ruler available. Be sure he has his handbook, *Math to Know,* and a calculator if he uses one at school. It's also a good idea to have a supply of crayons or colored pencils and a collection of small things, like buttons or coins, for acting out problems. Collections like these are called *manipulatives* at school.

Q: *Why should my daughter have a calculator? Isn't she supposed to be learning how to do calculations?*

A: Your daughter may be using a calculator at school, and a rule of thumb is to use calculators at home as they are used at school. Sometimes the main purpose of your daughter's homework may be to practice computing. For example, she may be learning to divide with decimals. Then she should do the assignment without a calculator. You might want to let her use the calculator to check her answers. She can then go back and redo any incorrect exercises.

Math, however, is not all calculations. Sometimes, the main purpose of an assignment is to practice solving complicated problems. For example, if the computation is messy and you can tell that the point of the homework is to practice choosing a formula and using it correctly, then she should use the calculator. Just be sure she does have the necessary skills to do the computation if she has to.

Q: *My son has no textbook. He just gets lots and lots of math worksheets. I'd like to help him review from time to time, or help him study for tests, but I am not even sure what topics he is studying or what topics he has studied. What can I do?*

A: Your child's teacher should have a curriculum guide listing the math topics to be taught at each grade. You might want to ask for a copy of this guide. Then, you and your son need to come up with an organized way to keep track of all of his math assignments. If your son has a three-ring binder, he can put all the loose papers in order in the binder. You may prefer to start a special binder or file at home to keep track of the completed and graded assignments.

Some teachers will keep graded homework and classwork in students' folders at school. If your son's teacher does this, ask to borrow the folder and make copies of your child's work. If assignments are sent home for you to sign and return, try to make copies or help your son write notes about the topic before returning the work to school. If you are really trying to be a tutor for your child, you both need to be able to refer to work he has done in order to choose topics for special study.

Making the Most of
HOMEWORK

Homework is often the most important tool a parent has for assessing a child's progress in math. It provides opportunities for a parent to act as tutor, role model, resource, and partner to the teacher.

Making the Most of
HOMEWORK

Q: *My son doesn't seem to know how to complete homework assignments. How can I help?*

A: The first step is to begin with your child's textbook. Find the pages which cover the topic of the homework. With your child, review the method described in the textbook. If he still does not understand, or if there is no textbook available, use the handbook, *Math to Know.* The handbook usually shows several ways to solve the same problem. One of the ways will probably be the one your son used in school. Try that method first, but he may prefer to use one of the other methods. Seeing a problem solved in different ways may also help him better understand the topic. If he likes an alternate method better, be sure to let his teacher know that you and your son agreed that, for him, this method works best.

The way you learned to solve similar problems may or may not help your child understand them. Try not to value one method that works over another method that works.

For example, *Math to Know* shows three different ways to do long division. (See page 189, pages 200–201, and pages 202–203.) One of the ways may work better for your son than the others. You may also find the way that matches the method you used in school.

Q: *Some of the terms in my child's textbook were not used when I was in school. How can I help my children when the math is not the same as the math I learned?*

A: You are right. Some of the terms used in math textbooks have changed. Some of the topics are new, too. You will find everything you need to know in *Math to Know*. The best place to start, when you don't know what a word means, is the Glossary of Mathematical Terms, which begins on page 442. Let your child see you looking up unfamiliar words—this is a good way to be a role model!

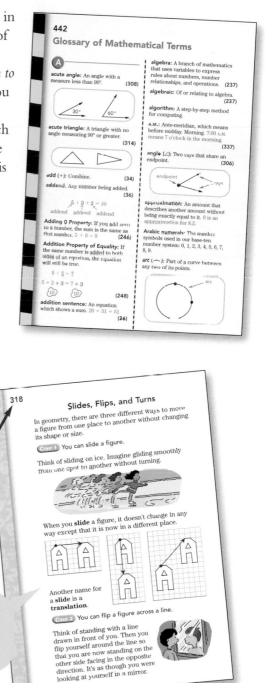

442
Glossary of Mathematical Terms

A

acute angle: An angle with a measure less than 90°. (308)

acute triangle: A triangle with no angle measuring 90° or greater. (314)

add (+): Combine. (34)

addend. Any number being added. (36)

$$5 + 3 + 2 = 10$$
addend addend addend

Adding 0 Property: If you add zero to a number, the sum is the same as that number. $5 + 0 = 5$ (246)

Addition Property of Equality: If the same number is added to both sides of an equation, the equation will still be true.
$$5 + 2 = 7$$
$$5 + 2 + 3 = 7 + 3$$
(248)

addition sentence: An equation which shows a sum. $20 + 31 = 51$ (36)

algebra: A branch of mathematics that uses variables to express rules about numbers, number relationships, and operations. (237)

algebraic: Of or relating to algebra. (237)

algorithm: A step-by-step method for computing.

A.M.: Ante-meridian, which means before midday. Morning. 7:00 A.M. means 7 o'clock in the morning. (337)

angle (∠): Two rays that share an endpoint. (306)

approximation: An amount that describes another amount without being exactly equal to it. 8 is an approximation for 8.3.

Arabic numerals: The number symbols used in our base-ten number system: 0, 1, 2, 3, 4, 5, 6, 7, 8, 9.

arc (⌢): Part of a curve between any two of its points.

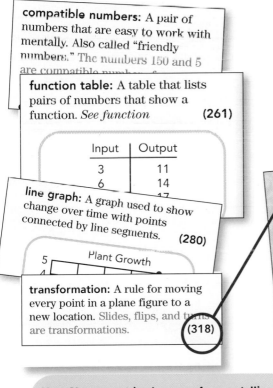

compatible numbers: A pair of numbers that are easy to work with mentally. Also called "friendly numbers." The numbers 150 and 5 are compatible numbers.

function table: A table that lists pairs of numbers that show a function. *See function* (261)

Input	Output
3	11
6	14

line graph: A graph used to show change over time with points connected by line segments. (280)

Plant Growth

transformation: A rule for moving every point in a plane figure to a new location. Slides, flips, and turns are transformations. (318)

318
Slides, Flips, and Turns

In geometry, there are three different ways to move a figure from one place to another without changing its shape or size.

Case 1 You can slide a figure.

Think of sliding on ice. Imagine gliding smoothly from one spot to another without turning.

When you **slide** a figure, it doesn't change in any way except that it is now in a different place.

Another name for a **slide** is a **translation**.

Case 2 You can flip a figure across a line.

Think of standing with a line drawn in front of you. Then you flip yourself around the line so that you are now standing on the other side facing in the opposite direction. It's as though you were looking at yourself in a mirror.

Most Glossary entries have a reference telling you where to go to find out more about that topic. To find out more about transformations, go to page 318 in *Math to Know*.

15

$Q\!:$ *How do I actually use the handbook? Should my daughter and I just read it together?*

$A\!:$ For some topics, looking up the topic and reading about it may be enough. But often you will want to rework the example step-by-step with your daughter. You may wish to use a separate piece of paper for each new problem. It is even a good idea to use a different color pencil or marker to show each step. As you work through the example, explain each step. Here is an example from page 177.

Computing with Whole Numbers and Decimals **177**

ANOTHER WAY You can also multiply by finding all the partial products, and then adding.

H T O
1 3 9
×   3
——
2 7 ← Multiply the ones. 3 × 9 ones = 27 ones
9 0 ← Multiply the tens. 3 × 3 tens = 9 tens
3 0 0 ← Multiply the hundreds. 3 × 1 hundred = 3 hundreds
——
4 1 7 ← Add the partial products.

MORE HELP See 175

ANOTHER WAY You can also multiply without listing the partial products.

H T O
1 2
1 3 9
×   3
——
4 1 7

Multiply the ones. 3 × 9 ones = 27 ones
Since 27 is 2 tens + 7 ones, write 7 in the ones place of the product and write 2 above the tens place, so that you will remember it.

Multiply the tens. 3 × 3 tens = 9 tens
Add the 9 tens to the 2 tens you already have. Since 11 tens is 1 hundred + 1 ten, write 1 in the place of the product and write 1 above the hundreds place, so that you will remember it.

Multiply the hundreds. 3 × 1 hundred = 3 hundreds
Add the 3 hundreds to the 1 hundred you have. Write 4 in the hundreds place of the product.

★ ANSWER: No matter which way you use, Dana needs 417 beads for 3 necklaces.

1 2
1 3 9
×   3
——
4 1 7

Q: *Sometimes my son brings home a worksheet that has small type and not enough space to really do the work. This is very frustrating for him. What should I do?*

A: Sometimes worksheets can be overwhelming. Try copying the problems onto another sheet of paper, leaving plenty of room for work. Sometimes having very little on a page can really help a child focus on a particular problem. Copying a problem onto a different piece of paper may also make it easier for your child to refer to examples or instructions that are not on the same side of the homework sheet as the problem. When you copy problems, be sure your child sees you double-check that you copied it correctly. Again, you are acting as a role model. Soon, your child should be comfortable copying the problems by himself.

If your child is not required to show his work, then be sure he places his answers in the appropriate spaces on the worksheet before turning it in.

21. $\dfrac{1}{2} + \dfrac{1}{4}$

$\dfrac{1 \times 2}{2 \times 2} \longrightarrow \dfrac{2}{4}$

$\dfrac{1}{4} \longrightarrow$

$+\dfrac{1}{4}$
_____
$\dfrac{3}{4}$

22. $\dfrac{2}{3} + \dfrac{1}{6}$

116 Fractions

Name _____ Date _____

Rewrite with like denominators. Add. Simplify.

21. $\frac{1}{2} + \frac{1}{4}$ 22. $\frac{2}{3} + \frac{1}{6}$ 23. $\frac{1}{5} + $

24. $\frac{1}{3} + \frac{2}{9}$ 25. $\frac{3}{8} + \frac{1}{4}$ 26.

27. $\frac{1}{2} + \frac{1}{10}$ 28. $\frac{1}{3} + \frac{1}{6}$

30. $\frac{2}{5} + \frac{1}{2}$ 31. $\frac{1}{4} + \frac{3}{8}$

Add. Write the sum in simplest form.

33. $1\frac{1}{4} + 2\frac{1}{4}$ 34. $2\frac{3}{8} + 3\frac{3}{8}$

36. $2\frac{1}{3} + 2\frac{3}{6}$ 37. $1\frac{4}{6} + 4\frac{1}{12}$ 38. $3\frac{1}{3} + 2\frac{1}{4}$

Q: *My daughter's work is so sloppy that I sometimes think this causes her to get wrong answers. What can I do?*

A: Try helping your daughter set up her paper before she gets started. Figure out how much space she will need for each problem. Be generous. Fold the paper into sections. If she has difficulty lining up the numbers when computing, try having her use graph paper or lined paper turned sideways. Also, encourage her to slow down and take the time required for neatness.

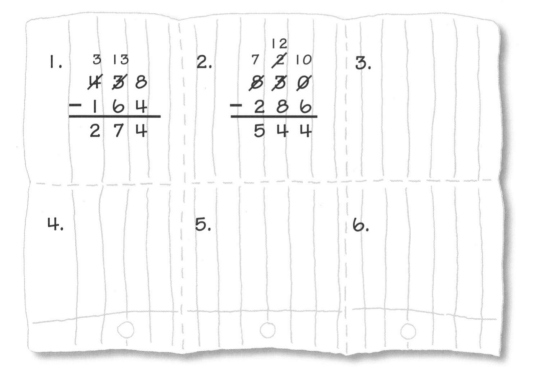

Q: *When my son asks me to check his homework, I find many answers that are wrong. How do I decide whether he has been careless or he does not understand the concepts?*

A: Try asking him to redo some of the problems that he got wrong. If he gets the correct answers this time, he was probably just careless. If he makes the same errors again, he probably does not understand the concept and should go back to his textbook or handbook for a review. If he successfully uses a method other than the one presented at school, it might be a good idea to send a note to the teacher explaining why he prefers the new method. In mathematics, there are often several good ways to solve the same problem.

Q: *Often, my daughter rushes through her math homework and makes an incredible number of careless errors. Then she asks me to find them all! How can I make her more responsible for her own work?*

A: First, try to convince her not to rush. Make sure that you are not accidentally encouraging her to rush by promising a treat *as soon as you finish your homework.* When she finishes, don't just tell her which answers are incorrect. Perhaps tell her how many are wrong or which row contains errors. Have her then check to find the incorrect answers. She may slow down and be more careful if she realizes that correcting careless mistakes takes more time than doing careful work to start with.

Can you find the two wrong answers in this row?

$Q:$ *My son says he wants me to help with his homework. But what he really wants is for me to do his homework! How much help should I give?*

$A:$ First, try to decide whether there is some non-math reason for his confusion. If he's overtired, change his homework time. If he wants to be doing something else, schedule that activity around his homework time.

If your son doesn't understand how to do the problems at all, take a new piece of paper and do the first one yourself. Use the method shown in the textbook if he has one. Show every step and explain what you are doing as you work. Then, remove the paper and ask your son to redo the same problem on his own homework paper, explaining each step as he goes along.

If he is still confused, try writing the problem on another piece of paper, this time leaving out parts of the solution. Have your son fill in the missing numbers. Above all, be patient and work with him, not for him.

If your son just doesn't seem to understand the method shown in the textbook, or wants to see other ways of solving the problem, look for a different method in the handbook and send a note to the teacher explaining your son's use of an alternate method. If, after all of this, you are both still stumped, work with your son to write a note to the teacher that clearly explains your problem and promises to complete the assignment as soon as the teacher has helped you clear up the problem. Include examples of the work you did with the note.

$$3 \overline{\smash{)}238} \quad 79 \text{ R } 1$$

Q: *My daughter is very independent and really doesn't want my help with her math homework. However, sometimes she thinks she understands the topic, but really she doesn't. What can I do?*

A: Independence can be a very good thing—you want your child to feel confident about her math skills. Don't discourage that. Give your daughter *Math to Know*. It is a great resource for parents and teachers, but it is written on a child's level and can certainly be used independently. When your daughter finishes her homework, ask her if you can check it over. Ask her how she solved some of the problems. This can be helpful just to see if she understands the general concept. If she does not want your help finding careless errors, leave this to the teacher. Just be sure she has the basic concepts. If not, send her back to the handbook.

Q: *What should I do if my son brings home so much math homework that he is just overwhelmed?*

A: First be sure that the homework is really intended to be done in one day. Often, teachers give assignments that are to be done over a period of a few days. If that is the case, help your son break the assignment into parts and write down which part he should do each day.

Q: *What if the assignment really is just one day's homework?*

A: First, be sure that your child's outside activities are not part of the problem. Next, understand that some students take longer to do certain assignments than others. Try cutting the assignment down. Be sure to include a few of each different type of problem. For example, if your son brings home addition and subtraction problems, choose some of each. Then write a note to the teacher explaining that the assignment was too long for your child and that he will complete the assignment the next night, or over the weekend.

If this is a consistent issue, you may wish to make an appointment for a teacher conference. The two of you can work as partners to make sure your child's homework is useful and can be done in a reasonable amount of time. Do not, however, expect the teacher to modify homework assignments just because your son has too many afterschool activities.

Q: *My daughter never brings home a textbook, just sheets of paper with exercises or problems. She finds it very confusing if I try to help her using a method different from the method she was shown in school. I'd like to at least start with the school's method, but she doesn't remember enough to describe it to me.*

A: Perhaps your daughter will be able to recognize the method she used in school when she looks up the topic in the handbook. If not, explain your situation to the teacher. The teacher may be able to have the students complete (and correct) one of each kind of problem on the homework sheet before leaving school. That will show you which method was presented in class.

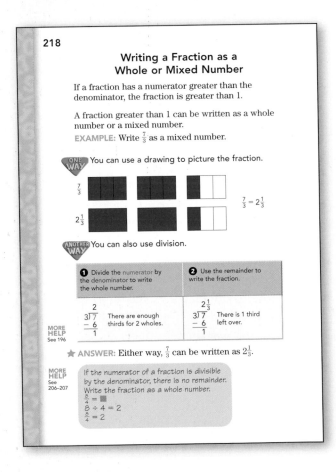

If your child struggles with that method, you should still look at the other methods shown in the handbook. Often, one of the methods provides a visual model that may make the mathematics more meaningful for your daughter.

For example, on pages 218 and 219, the first method gives a visual model to help students understand what is happening when you write a fraction as a mixed number or a mixed number as a fraction. The pictures should help make the concepts more real for your child.

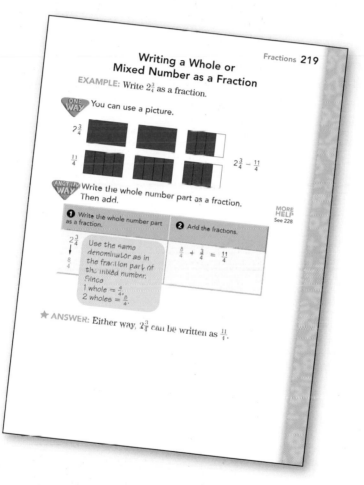

Q: *My daughter does not do well in math. But her teacher never sends home any homework. What should I do?*

A: Ask her teacher to send home the classwork she does in school. If there is a textbook, ask whether your daughter can take that home as well. Go over each type of problem your child has done. Ask her to explain how she got the answer. If she doesn't seem to understand, go first to her textbook. Try explaining what is in the book. If that doesn't seem to work, go to your handbook, *Math to Know*. You will find different ways to get the same answer. One of these other methods may make more sense to you and your daughter. If there is no textbook, you will be able to find all the instruction you need in the handbook.

Helping Your Child Prepare for
TESTS

Tests can sometimes be stressful for both students and parents. However, tests can also be a valuable resource for students, teachers, and parents. *Math to Know* offers a section on Test Taking Skills (see pages 408–413) which can help remove some of the stress so your children can do their best.

Helping Your Child Prepare for
TESTS

Q: *What is the best way to help my daughter prepare for a math test?*

A: The best way for you to help your child prepare for math tests is to encourage her to ask questions when she does not understand something. She should also keep up with all her homework assignments. Most of the questions on the test will be just like ones your child has seen before.

Keep assignments and quizzes in a notebook and try to review them regularly. Regular review and practice will likely be much more helpful than an intense study session just before an important test.

See pages 408 and 409 in *Math to Know* for additional tips on helping your child take tests.

Q: *What do I do when my son does poorly on a test?*

A: Ask the teacher to provide the correct answers if you are unsure about any of them. Go over each problem your son answered incorrectly. If he can solve the problems with no extra help, then he may be having trouble managing his time or concentrating during the test session. If this happens several times, talk with the teacher. Perhaps the two of you can find a way to keep time and anxiety from falsely indicating a poor understanding of the math.

When the math <u>is</u> the difficulty, work with your son, using *Math to Know* as a resource, until he can solve the problems he missed and others like them.

Some teachers allow students to retake tests on which they did poorly. Find out the teacher's policy on this.

Q: *What about standardized tests? How can I help my daughter prepare for those?*

A: Standardized tests assess all the math skills your child has learned since she started school. The best preparation is to be sure your daughter is keeping up in her regular math class.

It is not realistic to review all the math your child has been taught right before the standardized tests. What you can do is to make sure your daughter gets a good night's sleep and has a good breakfast before the test. Go over the tips for taking tests that are outlined on pages 408 and 409 in *Math to Know*. These will help your child perform her best and use her time efficiently.

How much time do I have to complete the test? Do all the questions count equally? Can I use my textbook, my handbook, my calculator, or notes? Does the teacher want explanations for short-answer test items?

Be sure your child is prepared for multiple-choice tests. It is important that she realizes that estimating and eliminating obviously wrong answer choices can be very helpful and are *not* cheating. Using these techniques shows a good understanding of math concepts. See pages 410 and 411 in *Math to Know* for tips on taking multiple-choice tests.

If your child is anxious about standardized tests, ask the teacher to send home some old tests for her to practice on.

Q: *Many tests, including some new standardized tests, ask children to explain their thinking. What is the best way to help my son prepare for these kinds of questions?*

A: The best way to prepare for these kinds of questions is to get your son into the habit of *talking math*. When he has math word problems to do, make a practice of asking questions like *How did you get this answer?* or *Why did you use multiplication?* Ask him to explain every step he took. If the two of you have worked through a problem together, you may wish to model this process by going back over the problem, describing each step you took, and then asking him to try doing the same. For this process, use the same problem, or change the numbers but not the words.

You can find a good sample of an "explain your thinking" problem on page 412 in *Math to Know.*

How did you solve this problem? Let's go through it, step-by-step.

Q: *My daughter does poorly on tests. She becomes very anxious that she may not have time to finish. So, she spends more time worrying about that than actually doing the problems. What can be done?*

A: If you are talking about routine classroom tests prepared by the teacher, time should not be an issue. Explain the problem to her teacher. Most teachers will allow extra time for students who need it. If your daughter knows she can have as much time as she needs, she may relax and concentrate better.

If you are talking about timed standardized tests, extra time may not be permitted unless your child has a diagnosed learning disability. There are, however, some steps you can take to help your child. Try to obtain copies of tests given in previous years. Time your daughter as she works through these and see how much of the test she is able to finish without panicking. Help her learn to pace herself. If there are 20 problems to be done in 10 minutes, have her think about doing the first ten or so in the first five minutes.

There may be other reasons your daughter is taking a long time to solve each problem:

- Perhaps she needs to brush up on her basic addition, subtraction, multiplication, and division facts.

- She may not be using a calculator even if it is allowed.

- Some problems may be solved in a more efficient way that your daughter is not aware of.

- Some problems only ask for an approximate answer rather than an exact answer. Using estimation skills on these can help save a great deal of time. Have your daughter look up "Estimation" in the index of *Math to Know* and study some of the pages listed there.

Bringing Math into
EVERYDAY LIFE

Children remember the math they use. Don't miss out on daily opportunities to help your child use math. Be a good role model for your child. Demonstrate how you use math every day.

Bringing Math into
EVERYDAY LIFE

$Q:$ *What kinds of math questions should I be asking?*

$A:$ Here are some examples of questions that you can ask to make your children aware that math is everywhere. Ideally, your children will soon begin to ask questions themselves. If they hesitate over the solution, model good problem-solving behavior by talking through a way to figure it out. Sometimes you may not know the answer. That's fine. Show your children how you, too, can use *Math to Know* as a resource.

Cooking

- How can we measure $2\frac{1}{2}$ cups of flour?

- This recipe makes two dozen cookies. How many cookies is that?

- I am putting the cookies in the oven at 1:15. They need to bake for 20 minutes. What time should I take them out?

Reading the newspaper

- What type of graph is this? What does the graph tell you?

- This ad shows some items on sale for half price. These jeans are originally $24, how much will they cost on sale?

- This headline says that there are 400 thousand people in our city. Is that more or less than a million?

- What do you think tomorrow's temperature will be?

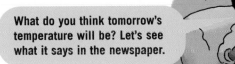

What do you think tomorrow's temperature will be? Let's see what it says in the newspaper.

Grocery shopping

- I need exactly two cups of tomato sauce. Will this 15-ounce can be enough?

- How much do you think these bananas weigh?

- Which eggs are the least expensive?

- This package of cheese weighs 0.65 (sixty-five hundredths of a) pound. Is that more or less than a pound?

How much do you think these bananas weigh?

You'll find that math is everywhere. Once you start thinking that way, you'll be amazed at how many questions will come to you. And remember, if you aren't sure of any of the answers, you and your child can look up the topic in *Math to Know* either right away or when you get home.

Q: *My fourth-grade son is having a lot of difficulty learning his multiplication and division facts. In fact, he is still having some trouble with his addition and subtraction facts. How can I help him memorize these facts?*

A: First of all, make sure he understands that there are strategies for learning the facts. He does not need to memorize every fact! For example, if he knows 3 + 8, he also knows 8 + 3. If you make a multiplication table to hang on the refrigerator or to use as a breakfast placemat, you can search for patterns for multiplying by 0, 1, 2, and 5. This can make those multiplication facts easy to learn. See pages 86–87 in *Math to Know* for some general tips on mastering basic facts.

Math to Know has a special section on fact strategies for each of the four operations. For addition, see pages 40–45; for subtraction, see pages 54–59; for multiplication, see pages 66–73; and for division, see pages 82–85.

Some facts may best be learned by just memorizing them. Try to think of a mnemonic, or memory device, to help your child with the facts he finds most difficult. For example, many children have difficulty with $7 \times 8 = 56$. Try writing this on a blank piece of paper and repeating it several times while your child notes the pattern.

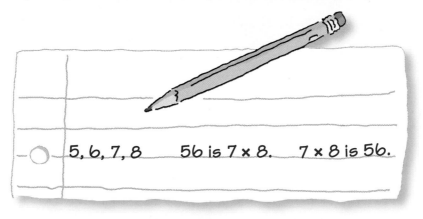

Think about posting a fact of the week on your refrigerator. At various times during the day, ask your child that particular fact, or better yet, ask: *What fact is on the refrigerator this week?*

Get the whole family involved in the fact of the week. Look for ways to use it as you do everyday things.

- Look at those 7 school buses. They each have 8 wheels! how many wheels is that?

- There are 8 people in front of us in this line. How long will we wait if each needs 7 minutes to check out?

You might offer a special reward at the end of the week if he can remember the fact.

To review facts and identify the troublesome ones, use index cards to make flash cards of all the facts. When your child is unable to recall a fact, make another card with that same fact and add it to the pile. Whenever possible, work with him to devise a mnemonic for that fact.

You might also make a deck of playing cards to use to practice facts. Make 13 sets of four cards that have the same answer, for example:

$$2 \times 3 \qquad 4 + 2 \qquad 10 - 4$$

$$36 \div 6$$

Play any of your favorite card games (like War or Go Fish) using these cards. Consider having a family game night and involve the whole family and some friends as well!

Do you have any cards with a value of 6?

Q: *With three children in the family, we seem to be always rushing around. How can I find the time to stop and bring out the math in a situation?*

A: Use time that might otherwise be wasted, like the time you spend waiting in line at the grocery store checkout or driving from one place to another. You can also think about math while you are rushing around. Ask questions like these.

- I only have $20 in my wallet. Is that enough to fill the gas tank?
- These granola bars cost $4.79. If I give the clerk $5, what coins will I get back?
- How long do you think it will take us to get through this traffic light?
- What do you think will be the total cost of all these groceries?
- I'm driving 30 miles per hour, how long will it take me to drive one mile?

Thinking About Why Your Child May Be
STRUGGLING

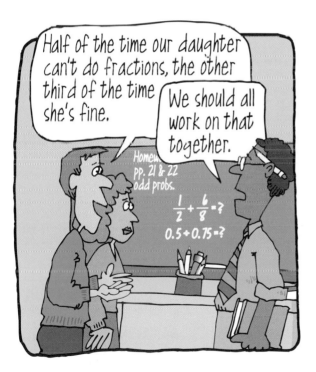

There can be many reasons why a child may be having difficulty with mathematics. Trying to figure out exactly what the problem is can be like trying to solve a puzzle. If your child is struggling, it is important that you play the role of partner to the teacher.

Thinking About Why Your Child May Be STRUGGLING

Q: **My son says he doesn't like math. What should I do?**

A: Nobody likes to fail. Help your child meet with some success. Look in the handbook to find another way to solve problems that are troublesome. Ask lots of questions you know he can answer. Show him he really does know something about math. Talk to his teacher about ways you can help.

Try to be enthusiastic about math. If you didn't like math when you were in school, or didn't do well in math, don't let your son think that makes it OK for him not to try. Do help him see that everyone bumps into things that are hard to do and the best way to get past the rough spots is to spend some time on them.

Use the handbook. You will find the clear, step-by-step approach helpful. Your child should also enjoy the informal style of the handbook. The Math Alerts will help him avoid mistakes before he makes them.

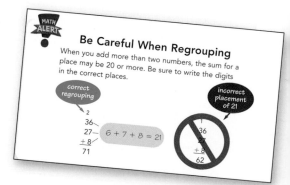

MATH ALERT

Be Careful When Regrouping

When you add more than two numbers, the sum for a place may be 20 or more. Be sure to write the digits in the correct places.

correct regrouping

$$
\begin{array}{r}
2 \\
36 \\
27 \\
+\,8 \\
\hline
71
\end{array}
$$

$6 + 7 + 8 = 21$

incorrect placement of 21

$$
\begin{array}{r}
1 \\
36 \\
27 \\
+\,8 \\
\hline
62
\end{array}
$$

Do not ask him to do pages of drill and practice that have not been assigned in school. That may make him like math even less. Help him with his homework. If you would like him to practice math at home, use activities and games. Your son's teacher will be able to suggest some good ones. Also, don't forget about board games or card games.

Q: *My daughter seems to have good years and bad years. Sometimes she does very well in math and sometimes she just doesn't do well at all. What might be the reason?*

A: Teachers have different teaching styles, and students have different learning styles. Many children learn best by visual methods. Reading about math in a book often works well for these students. Other students learn best by *auditory* methods. They learn most from the teacher's explanation. Other children learn best by *tactile* methods. They need to use real materials that they can pick up and move around. Think about what worked best during her good years, then, talk to your daughter's teacher and see whether he or she can find the learning style that works best for your daughter. Then both of you can provide your daughter with help that best matches that style.

$\frac{1}{2}$ of 12 is 6.

When this year is almost over, talk to the principal about your daughter's learning style. The principal is aware of the many different teaching styles. Knowing your daughter's learning style will make it easier for the principal to place her in a class for the next school year. After a few weeks of the new year, meet with the teacher to discuss whether the teaching and learning styles are a good fit.

Q: **My son doesn't understand the math in his textbook. He needs more hands-on work. How can I help at home?**

A: You can use the handbook to help make math real for your child. You will notice that many of the concepts in *Math to Know* are introduced using a mathematical picture or model. You might try using these models to help your child with topics he is studying in school. For example, you might use pennies or buttons as counters to help your child understand division. Pages 78 and 79 in *Math to Know* will show you all the steps.

78

Ways to Divide

There are many ways to find a quotient. Use a method that works best for you.

Using Counters to Divide

You can act out a division problem by using counters.

Case 1 You can use counters to find the number in each group.

EXAMPLE 1: Brad has 12 rabbits. He puts the same number of rabbits into each of 4 cages. How many rabbits does Brad put in each cage?

Think: $12 \div 4 = \blacksquare$

❶ Use 12 counters to stand for the 12 rabbits.

❷ Place them one-by-one into 4 groups, which is the number of cages.

❸ Count how many are in each group.

There are 3 in each group.
$12 \div 4 = 3$

★ ANSWER: Brad puts 3 rabbits in each cage.

You will also probably be surprised at how many math materials you have right at home. In *Math to Know*, you will see blocks to show hundreds, tens, and ones. You probably don't have those at home. How about using dollar bills, dimes, and pennies? These will help your child get a better understanding of place value and addition and subtraction of larger numbers. When your son runs out of pennies while subtracting ones, he can trade one of his dimes for 10 pennies. If he runs out of dimes, he can trade one dollar for ten dimes.

When your child is studying fractions, pull out your measuring cups and rulers.

Q: *My daughter does very well on computation exercises, but when it comes to word problems she has a lot of trouble. Do you have some suggestions?*

A: Don't ignore the problem, hoping it will fix itself. First, decide whether she has difficulty understanding what she reads in other subjects. If that is the case, talk to her teacher about ways to improve her reading comprehension.

If the problem is limited to word problems in math, she may be having difficulty working through a problem step-by-step. She may be trying to get the answer too quickly. *Math to Know* includes a whole section just on Problem Solving. (See pages 364–400.) Here your daughter can find many problems that have been worked out step-by-step. She should try to imitate the steps when solving word problems on her own.

She may also be unsure when to use each of the basic operations: addition, subtraction, multiplication, and division. When you use each of these operations in your daily life, try to point them out to her.

I am spending money. That's taking it away from the money I have in the bank, so, I need to subtract the amount of that check from my bank balance.

Q: *Sometimes, when my son is working on a new topic, he finds he needs some skills he has forgotten. What can he do?*

A: *Math to Know* can help him here. He can either use the handbook to look up the skills he's forgotten, or look up the new topic. **MORE HELP** references tell where he can go to review the skills he needs.

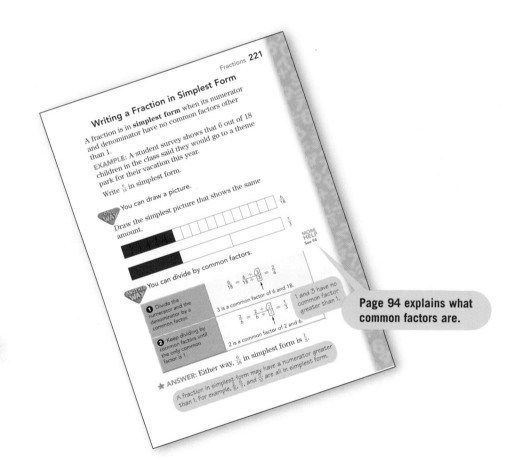

Page 94 explains what common factors are.

Q: *My daughter has been having difficulty since the first grade. She has fallen so far behind that she really doesn't understand any of the math her teacher is presenting. Is there any way she can catch up?*

A: If your daughter's skills are several years behind, she may need some help outside of the regular classroom. You are right that it will be difficult for her to understand the work being taught at her grade level. Talk to your child's teacher as soon as you can. The sooner she is able to receive some extra help, the sooner she will be able to catch up.

$Q:$ *My son seems to be having more trouble lately than ever before. Do you have any ideas about what might be the problem?*

$A:$ Try to think about what may be going on that is different. Maybe your child needs glasses or a new prescription for his glasses. Perhaps the solution to your problem can be as simple as that.

Your child may have a problem paying attention. Sometimes, as math concepts become more difficult, attention problems can become more obvious. Ask your son's teacher whether he seems to be listening or if something seems to be distracting him. You might want to arrange for your child to sit in a place with fewer distractions, closer to the teacher. If the teacher is aware of the problem, he or she can help your son to focus his attention when his mind seems to be wandering.

Q: *I'm not exactly sure how to approach the teacher. I don't want her to think I am blaming her for my daughter's poor math performance. Should I just wait until she contacts me?*

A: It is best to discuss the problem as soon as possible. The teacher may be waiting until scheduled parent conferences. Meanwhile, the problem is not likely to go away. Also, time is often very limited during a formal conference.

If it is early in the year, the teacher may not be aware of the weaknesses of each student. If you highlight your daughter's difficulty, the teacher will begin to focus specifically on her, and you may be able to solve the problem sooner. There will be almost a whole year to make progress.

When you are ready to speak to the teacher, be sure to make an appointment. Don't try to talk about problems when you are at school dropping off or picking up your child.

The focus of the conversation should be on finding the best way for your child to progress in math. If you concentrate on that and compliment her on things about her class that have worked out well for your child, the teacher will not think you are there to evaluate her performance as a teacher. Listen carefully to how she describes your child. Your daughter may behave very differently at school than at home. You both have a lot to share and together you should be able to work out a plan that will increase your daughter's success in mathematics.

NOTES